JUSTIN THYME

The Depressed Entrepreneur

Copyright © 2024 by Justin Thyme

All rights reserved. No part of this publication may be reproduced, stored or transmitted in any form or by any means, electronic, mechanical, photocopying, recording, scanning, or otherwise without written permission from the publisher. It is illegal to copy this book, post it to a website, or distribute it by any other means without permission.

First edition

This book was professionally typeset on Reedsy.
Find out more at reedsy.com

Contents

1	Introduction: You Are Not Alone	1
2	My Personal Journey	3
3	1.1 Identifying Emotional and Physical Red Flags	6
4	1.2 Recognizing Work-Related Triggers	11
5	1.3 Self-Assessment: Understanding When Help is Needed	17
6	2.1 The Unique Mental Burdens of Entrepreneurship	24
7	2.2 How Entrepreneurship Impacts Personal Relationships	32
8	2.3 The Biological and Psychological Aspects of Depression	40
9	3.1 Building a Healthy Work-Life Balance	48
10	3.2 Managing Stress through Daily Habits	56
11	3.3 Professional Resources for Mental Health Support	64
12	4.1 Cultivating Resilience in the Face of Setbacks	72
13	4.2 Redefining Success Beyond Business Metrics	80
14	4.3 Sustaining Mental Health for the Long Haul	88
15	Moving Forward with Balance and Strength	96

1

Introduction: You Are Not Alone

A certain loneliness comes with being an entrepreneur, a sense of isolation that gnaws at you when the world sees only your successes, while inside, you struggle to keep afloat. You may feel overwhelmed, burnt out, and, worst of all, disconnected from your own sense of well-being. If you've found yourself waking up with a heavy heart, unsure how to keep moving forward while steering your business, I want you to know this: you are not alone.

As entrepreneurs, we're wired to hustle. We're taught to keep going no matter what—push through the pain, meet the deadline, make the sale. But there comes a point when the hustle takes more than it gives. And suddenly, you're no longer in control of the very thing you've worked so hard to build—your mind. It clouds over, making decisions is harder, dampening your motivation, and twisting the joy of creation into something you barely recognize.

But having a clear mind is vital, and not just for the sake of your business. Your mental clarity is what allows you to innovate, to lead, to adapt. It's the very thing that fuels your business's growth, and more importantly, your own growth as a person. Without it, you're just going through the motions, operating in survival mode instead of thriving.

I know because I've been there. I've sat in front of my desk, staring blankly at the same to-do list I couldn't find the energy to tackle. I've felt the weight of the world on my shoulders, pretending everything was fine when inside, I was falling apart. And I'm still on this journey. This book isn't coming from a place of complete recovery, but from the trenches. I'm walking this path alongside you, learning how to manage my mind while growing my business, every single day.

This is my personal journey of recognizing the signs, accepting the struggle, and, little by little, finding ways to navigate through it. And it's the journey I hope to walk with you in these pages. Together, we'll explore what it means to be an entrepreneur who struggles with mental health but refuses to let it define us.

If you've ever felt alone in this battle, I want to reassure you that you don't have to fight it in silence. There's a way to manage your mind while still building the business you're passionate about. And it starts here, with understanding that it's okay to not be okay. It's okay to admit that you're struggling. And **it's okay to seek help**.

This is not just a guide to overcoming the challenges you face as a business owner—it's a companion for those moments when you feel like you're losing yourself. It's a reminder that you have the strength to manage both your mind and your business. And above all, it's a promise that you are not alone.

2

My Personal Journey

It's been 2,200 days since my life took a turn I never saw coming. When I first started this journey, I was full of hope, ambition, and determination. I believed that no obstacle was too big, no setback too severe. But life has a way of humbling you, breaking down those illusions of invincibility. In these past six years, I've been forced to face more than I ever imagined. And 60 days ago, my business—my pride and joy—came to an end. I had to make the hardest decision of my life and close the doors, terminating the staff who had become like family to me.

There's a special kind of heartbreak that comes with watching something you've poured your soul into slowly fall apart. For years, I fought to keep things together, doing everything I could to push through the challenges. But the truth is, I was already breaking long before the business did. Behind the scenes, my back had literally given out—a debilitating injury that would've been enough to knock anyone down. On top of that, I carried the weight of unresolved trauma and a deepening depression that refused to let go.

Yet, here I am. Still standing. Some days, it feels like I'm just surviving, like I'm clinging to the edge of something too steep to climb. But I'm here. I'm soldiering on, one day at a time, because that's what you do when there's no other choice. You keep going, even when it feels like every step is taken in the dark, even when the burden feels too heavy to carry alone.

I'm not going to sugarcoat it—these past 60 days have been some of the hardest of my life. Shutting down the business felt like admitting defeat, like losing a piece of myself. And the physical pain, mixed with the emotional toll of depression, has made it difficult to even recognize who I am anymore. But in the midst of all this, I've realized something important: sometimes, survival is enough. Sometimes, simply waking up and deciding to keep moving forward is the bravest thing you can do.

I'm still here, not because I have it all figured out, but because I refuse to give up. I know the path ahead won't be easy. There are still so many unresolved issues to face, and recovery—both physical and mental—feels like a distant goal. But if there's one thing I've learned, it's that strength doesn't always look like we imagine it will. It's not about charging ahead without fear or conquering every challenge with ease. Sometimes, it's about continuing to show up, no matter how hard things get.

This journey I'm on is far from over. I'm still battling the depression that lingers like a shadow, still working through the pain, still trying to heal from wounds I've carried for too long. But I'm determined to keep going, because I believe that even in the darkest moments, there's hope. And I want you to know that if you're going through something similar, you're not alone in this. We can keep going together, one step at a time.

So, welcome to the journey. This path may not be easy, and there will be moments when it feels overwhelming, but you don't have to walk it alone. Together, we can navigate the highs and lows, the setbacks and small victories. We'll learn how to manage our minds while rebuilding our businesses, our lives, and ourselves. I invite you to take this journey with me, side by side, as we figure out how to heal, grow, and find our way forward. Let's take it one day at a time—together.

3

1.1 Identifying Emotional and Physical Red Flags

Common Emotional Indicators of Depression

Depression isn't always easy to recognize, especially when you're in the midst of running a business. It can disguise itself as exhaustion, a bad day, or simply the weight of responsibility. But there are emotional signs that often point to something deeper at play. Recognizing these signs is the first step toward managing your mental health while balancing the pressures of entrepreneurship.

One of the most common indicators is **persistent sadness or anxiety**. You might wake up with a heavy feeling in your chest or a sense of dread that never fully lifts. It's not just feeling down on occasion—this sadness lingers, hanging over your head like a cloud. Even in moments that should bring happiness, you find it hard to shake that weight, and your mind races with anxious thoughts, even when there's no immediate crisis.

Another telltale sign is the **loss of interest in activities you** *once enjoyed*. Remember when you used to feel excited about your work, your hobbies, or even spending time with friends and family? When depression takes hold, that excitement fades. You may start avoiding the very things that once made you feel alive—whether it's a favourite pastime, a business project you once loved, or even simply engaging with those closest to you. It's as if everything that used to bring you joy has lost its colour.

Perhaps most overwhelming is the sense of *feeling hopeless or completely overwhelmed*. This can show up as a constant feeling that no matter how hard you try, things are spiraling out of control. You might find yourself questioning your decisions, your abilities, and even your worth as an entrepreneur and a person. It's as if the mountain in front of you keeps getting steeper, and you can't see the way up. You're trying to keep everything together, but the weight feels unbearable.

These emotions aren't just fleeting—they're indicators that your mental health needs attention. They're signals that something deeper is happening and recognizing them is the first step toward healing. If you've been experiencing any of these feelings, you're not alone. It's okay to acknowledge what you're going through, and it's okay to reach out for help. Together, we can work on managing these emotions and taking back control, one step at a time.

Physical Symptoms Tied to Mental Health

While depression primarily affects the mind, its impact is often felt throughout the body. The connection between mental and physical health is profound, and depression can manifest in ways that leave you feeling drained, exhausted, and out of balance. Recognizing these physical symptoms is crucial because they're often the first clues that something deeper is affecting your well-being.

One of the most common physical symptoms is ***fatigue and low energy***. It's more than just being tired after a long day of work. This kind of fatigue feels pervasive, no matter how much rest you get. You wake up feeling exhausted, dragging yourself through the day with a sense that you're running on empty. Tasks that used to be routine now feel monumental, and even small responsibilities can seem like insurmountable hurdles. Your body feels as heavy as your mind, and getting through the day becomes an exhausting battle.

Another red flag is ***sleep disturbances***, which can take many forms. For some, it shows up as insomnia—lying awake at night, unable to shut off racing thoughts, staring at the clock while hours slip away. No matter how tired you are, sleep just won't come. On the other hand, depression can lead to ***oversleeping***, where you find yourself spending excessive time in bed, using sleep as a way to escape the weight of your emotions. Neither extreme brings real rest, leaving you feeling just as tired when you wake up as when you went to sleep.

Finally, ***appetite changes or fluctuations in weight*** often accompany depression. You may find yourself losing interest in food altogether, skipping meals without even realising it, as your appetite disappears. Or, you might experience the opposite, turning to food for comfort, eating more than usual in an attempt to fill an emotional void. Whether it's loss of appetite or overeating, these changes can lead to noticeable weight fluctuations, adding another layer of discomfort to what you're already feeling emotionally.

These physical symptoms are the body's way of signaling that something is wrong. When your mind is in turmoil, your body often follows suit, making it harder to cope with both the emotional and physical weight of depression. But the key is recognizing these signs and understanding that they're connected to your mental health. It's not just "in your head"—your body is feeling it too. And while it may seem overwhelming, addressing these physical symptoms can be a vital part of your journey toward healing and recovery.

Behavioral Signs That Things Aren't Right

Depression often sneaks into your life through subtle changes in behaviour. At first, you might not even notice the shift, but over time, these behaviour's can become red flags that something deeper is going on. As an entrepreneur, the demands on your time and attention are constant, but when your mental health starts to decline, the way you handle your day-to-day life begins to unravel.

One of the most telling signs is ***withdrawal from social or business engagements***. You may start avoiding networking events, meetings, or even casual get-together's with friends and family. Things that once felt energising or even necessary now feel overwhelming and draining. You find yourself pulling back, isolating yourself from others, not because you don't care, but because you just don't have the energy to be present. The thought of interacting with others feels too much, and it's easier to disappear into the background, hoping no one notices.

Another key indicator is ***difficulty focusing on work or making decisions***. The sharpness you once relied on to run your business seems to fade, replaced by a constant sense of brain fog. Tasks that used to be second nature now feel daunting, and even simple decisions can leave you feeling paralyzed. Whether it's figuring out the next step in a project or deciding what to prioritise in your day, you find yourself stuck, unable to move forward with the clarity and confidence you once had. Your focus drifts, and productivity takes a hit, adding to the frustration and sense of failure that depression often brings.

Finally, ***avoiding important tasks and responsibilities*** becomes a common pattern. You might start putting off things that need to get done—whether it's responding to emails, following up with clients, or handling financial matters. Procrastination takes over, not because you don't care, but because the weight of everything feels too heavy. Important deadlines slip by, responsibilities pile up, and soon, you're in a cycle of avoidance that only adds to your stress and anxiety.

These behavioural signs aren't just normal lapses in discipline or motivation. They're signals that your mental health is affecting the way you function in both your personal and professional life. Recognizing these patterns is crucial because they point to a larger issue that needs attention. It's not about blaming yourself for the changes—it's about understanding that when your mind is struggling, your behaviour will naturally follow suit. But with awareness comes the ability to take steps toward managing these symptoms and regaining control, little by little.

4

1.2 Recognizing Work-Related Triggers

The Pressure of Constant Decision-Making

As an entrepreneur, decision-making is an integral part of your daily life. Every choice you make, no matter how small, feels like it carries the weight of your entire business. The pressure to always make the right decision can be overwhelming, and it's a burden that often goes unnoticed by those who don't walk the same path. But for those of us who do, the constant need to decide can feel like an ever-present storm gathering overhead.

One of the greatest sources of this pressure is the ***weight of responsibility for your business's success***. When you're the one in charge, every decision seems to hold the fate of your business in its hands. It's not just about the day-to-day operations—it's about the livelihoods of your staff, the satisfaction of your clients, and the future of something you've worked tirelessly to build. That weight can be crushing, and the longer you carry it, the harder it becomes to ignore the strain it places on your mental and emotional health.

Alongside that responsibility is the ***fear of failure and financial instability***. Every decision you make feels like a step toward success or a potential misstep that could bring everything crashing down. The fear of failing—not just for yourself but for everyone depending on you—it can be paralysing. And behind that fear often lurks the anxiety about financial stability. The uncertainty of whether you'll be able to keep things afloat, meet payroll, or cover expenses adds a constant layer of stress, making it hard to focus on anything beyond just surviving the next day.

Then there's the **toll of working long hours without balance**. In an effort to keep things running smoothly, you may find yourself burning the candle at both ends, sacrificing personal time, relationships, and even your health. The line between work and life blurs until it doesn't exist at all, and suddenly, every waking hour revolves around your business. Without rest or balance, the relentless decision-making process wears you down. Your mind becomes fatigued, and decisions that once felt simple now feel impossible to make with clarity. The toll isn't just on your business; it's on you, too.

The constant pressure to make the right decisions can slowly erode your well-being, leaving you exhausted and uncertain. But recognizing this pressure is key. It's important to realise that even though it may feel like you're shouldering everything alone, there are ways to lighten the load. Finding balance, asking for support, and acknowledging that no one can get every decision right all the time are crucial steps toward managing the mental strain. It's a difficult path, but you don't have to walk it alone.

Isolation in the Entrepreneurial Journey

One of the most challenging aspects of being an entrepreneur is the *isolation* that often comes with it. As you pour yourself into building and growing your business, the support network that might have once surrounded you can start to fade, leaving you feeling alone in your struggles. While entrepreneurship is often romanticised as a path to freedom and success, the reality is that it can also be a lonely road.

A major factor contributing to this isolation is the *lack of a support network or sounding board*. When you're at the top, it's easy to feel like you have to have all the answers. There may not be many people you can confide in about the hard decisions you're facing, the doubts creeping into your mind, or the fears you have about the future of your business. You might not feel comfortable discussing these challenges with your employees or even your loved ones, and without a safe space to vent or seek advice, that burden grows heavier.

This isolation is compounded by *minimal connection with peers who truly understand the entrepreneurial journey.* It's difficult for someone who hasn't walked this path to fully grasp the unique pressures you face—constant decision-making, financial instability, and the fear of failure. While friends or family may offer sympathy, they might not have the insight to truly relate to the emotional and mental toll of entrepreneurship. Without the camaraderie of other business owners who have experienced these same highs and lows, it's easy to feel like you're navigating uncharted waters alone.

And as the demands of your business grow, it often leads

to ***disconnection from friends and family***, not out of choice, but out of necessity. Long hours at the office, late nights spent problem-solving, and a relentless focus on your work can slowly chip away at your personal relationships. You may miss important events, cancel plans, or simply be too exhausted to engage with those you care about. Over time, this can create a divide between you and the people who once provided emotional support, leaving you further isolated in your entrepreneurial journey.

This sense of isolation can be overwhelming, but it doesn't have to be permanent. Acknowledging that you feel alone is the first step toward reconnecting—with others and with yourself. It's important to remember that there are others out there who understand your struggles, and finding ways to build or rebuild that support network can make all the difference. Whether it's through joining entrepreneurial communities, seeking mentorship, or simply making time to reconnect with loved ones, breaking the cycle of isolation is possible. You don't have to face this journey in solitude.

Unclear Boundaries Between Personal Life and Work

For many entrepreneurs, the line between work and personal life becomes almost invisible. The passion you have for your business often leads to an all-consuming focus, where everything else falls by the wayside. What starts as dedication can slowly morph into a situation where there are ***unclear boundaries*** between your personal time and your professional responsibilities. And as those boundaries blur, the effects on your well-being and relationships become harder to ignore.

One of the most common signs of these blurred lines is

working during personal or family time. You may find yourself answering emails at the dinner table, taking work calls during a child's event, or staying up late to finish tasks that could have waited. What's meant to be a time for relaxation and connection with loved ones turns into another opportunity to catch up on work. This constant merging of work and home life can strain relationships, leaving you physically present but emotionally and mentally elsewhere.

Then, there's the ***feeling of guilt*** that comes with taking any time off. As an entrepreneur, you may feel like you're never truly "off the clock." When you do manage to take a break, you might be haunted by the thought that you should be working, that things will fall apart without your constant attention. The idea of stepping away, even briefly, feels like a risk—one you can't afford to take. Instead of enjoying time to rest and recharge, you're filled with anxiety and guilt, convinced that downtime is a luxury you haven't earned.

This guilt and over-commitment to work often leads to ***neglecting hobbies and self-care***. The activities that once brought you joy and helped you decompress take a back seat to your business. Exercise routines, creative outlets, or even simple self-care practices like reading a book or going for a walk become rare occurrences. Over time, this neglect of yourself not only diminishes your happiness but also erodes your energy and mental resilience. Without these moments of personal care, the line between work and personal life becomes even harder to distinguish, leaving you feeling drained and disconnected from the things that once made you feel whole.

Unclear boundaries between work and life don't just affect your business—they affect you, your health, and your relationships. Recognizing this imbalance is the first step toward reclaiming that personal space. It's not about abandoning your business; it's about giving yourself permission to step back, to rest, and to remember that you are more than just the work you do. Setting clear boundaries doesn't make you less dedicated—it makes you more sustainable as both an entrepreneur and a person.

5

1.3 Self-Assessment: Understanding When Help is Needed

How to Self-Evaluate Your Mental Health

As an entrepreneur, it's easy to get so wrapped up in running your business that you lose sight of your own well-being. But being able to *self-evaluate your mental health* is a critical skill, one that can help you recognize when something isn't quite right before it reaches a breaking point. Regularly checking in with yourself—just as you would with your business—is key to staying mentally healthy, especially when life becomes overwhelming.

One of the most effective ways to do this is by *tracking your emotional and behavioural patterns over time*. Pay attention to your mood, energy levels, and how you're feeling day to day. Are you constantly feeling down, anxious, or stressed? Are you pulling back from activities you once enjoyed or avoiding interactions you once embraced? **Start by keeping a mental or physical log of these changes**. Small shifts might not seem like much at first, but over time, they can add up to a clearer picture of how you're really doing. This allows you to spot patterns and recognize when negative emotions are becoming more than just occasional rough patches.

Another important sign to watch for is ***noticing negative thought spirals***. We all experience self-doubt or frustration from time to time, but when those thoughts start to spiral into a pattern of persistent negativity, it's a signal that your mental health may be struggling. You might catch yourself thinking, "I'm not good enough," "Everything is going wrong," or "I'll never be able to fix this." These thoughts can quickly snowball into a larger narrative of hopelessness and failure if left unchecked. By recognizing when your mind is stuck in these negative loops, you can interrupt the spiral and take steps to challenge those thoughts before they take over.

Lastly, an effective way to self-evaluate is by ***comparing your current well-being to previous mental states***. Think back to a time when you felt more balanced, energised, or content. How do you feel now in comparison? Have you been able to maintain that sense of well-being, or has it slipped? By reflecting on your past mental health, you can identify areas where things may have shifted and take note of what has changed in your life or routine that might be contributing to your current state. This comparison can provide valuable insight, helping you identify when you might need to seek support or make adjustments in your lifestyle to regain your mental balance.

Regular self-evaluation is a powerful tool in maintaining your mental health, especially in the fast-paced, high-pressure world of entrepreneurship. The more you track your emotions, challenge negative thoughts, and reflect on your well-being, the better equipped you'll be to recognize when it's time to make changes, reach out for help, or take a step back to care for yourself.

When to Seek Professional Help

As you navigate the complexities of entrepreneurship, it's crucial to recognize that seeking help is not a sign of weakness, but a vital step in managing your mental health. Understanding when to reach out for professional support can be life-changing. Here's a guide on how to know when it's time to seek help and the role that mental health professionals can play in your journey.

The Role of Therapy and Counseling in Managing Mental Health

Therapy and counseling can provide a safe space for you to explore your thoughts, feelings, and behaviours without judgment. A skilled therapist can help you identify patterns, develop coping strategies, and cultivate resilience in the face of challenges. They can guide you through the process of understanding your emotions, re-framing negative thoughts, and improving your overall mental well-being. Engaging in therapy can be particularly beneficial for entrepreneurs, as it allows you to discuss the unique pressures of running a business in a supportive environment. A professional can help you navigate not only your emotional landscape but also the practical aspects of your entrepreneurial journey.

Recognizing When Burnout Turns into Clinical Depression

Burnout can feel all-consuming, characterised by exhaustion, detachment, and a diminished sense of accomplishment. However, it's essential to recognize when burnout crosses the line into clinical depression. If you find that your feelings of hopelessness, fatigue, or disinterest in life persist for weeks or months, it may be a sign that you need professional help. Clinical depression often comes with additional symptoms, such as significant changes in appetite or sleep patterns, feelings of worthlessness, or difficulty concentrating. If you're experiencing these symptoms consistently, it's important to seek help before the situation escalates. Ignoring these signs can prolong your suffering and hinder your ability to effectively manage your business and personal life.

How to Find a Mental Health Professional Specialized in Entrepreneurship

Finding the right mental health professional can make a significant difference in your journey. Look for therapists or counselors who specialize in working with entrepreneurs or small business owners. They will have a deeper understanding of the unique challenges you face and can provide tailored support. Start by researching local therapists or online platforms that focus on entrepreneurship. You can also seek recommendations from your network, professional organizations, or entrepreneurial communities. Many mental health professionals offer initial consultations, which can help you determine if their approach aligns with your needs and comfort level.

Taking the step to seek professional help is a courageous and necessary part of managing your mental health as an entrepreneur. Remember, you don't have to navigate this journey alone. There are resources available to support you, and reaching out for help can pave the way for healing, growth, and renewed passion for your work. Prioritising your mental health is not only essential for your well-being, but it's also crucial for the success of your business. Embrace the journey toward healing and understand that you deserve the support and care that can help you thrive.

Early Interventions to Try at Home

When it comes to managing your mental health, taking proactive steps can make a significant difference. While professional help is invaluable, there are early interventions you can implement at home to begin the healing process and regain your mental clarity. Here are a few effective strategies to consider:

Mindfulness Exercises to Gain Clarity

In the whirlwind of running a business, it's easy to become overwhelmed by stress and anxiety. Mindfulness exercises can help you center your thoughts and gain clarity amid the chaos. Simple practices, such as deep breathing, meditation, or guided visualization, can be incredibly effective. Start with just a few minutes each day—find a quiet space, close your eyes, and focus on your breath. As thoughts arise, acknowledge them without judgment and gently bring your focus back to your breathing.

Over time, these exercises can help you cultivate a greater sense of calm, reduce stress, and improve your overall mental clarity. Integrating mindfulness into your daily routine can also help you develop a deeper awareness of your emotional and physical state, enabling you to respond to challenges with a clearer mind.

Journaling to Identify Negative Patterns

Journaling can be a powerful tool for self-reflection and awareness. Take a few moments each day to write down your thoughts, feelings, and experiences. This practice can help you identify negative patterns, recurring thoughts, or emotional triggers that may be affecting your mental health. Ask yourself guiding questions such as, "What am I feeling today?" or "What thoughts are weighing me down?" By putting pen to paper, you create an opportunity to process your emotions and gain insight into your mental state. Over time, you may notice patterns that can inform your decision-making and help you recognize when it's time to take a step back or seek additional support.

Small Adjustments to Workload and Routine

Sometimes, the pressure of entrepreneurship can be alleviated with small, intentional adjustments to your workload and routine. Begin by assessing your current responsibilities and identifying areas where you can lighten your load. Consider delegating tasks, outsourcing specific projects, or prioritising your most critical objectives. Additionally, evaluate your daily routine—are there times when you can integrate breaks or moments of self-care? Establishing boundaries around your work hours can help ensure you're not constantly available, allowing you to carve out time for rest and personal activities. Small adjustments can lead to a significant reduction in stress, helping you regain balance and clarity in your life.

Implementing these early interventions at home can be a crucial step toward managing your mental health as an entrepreneur. By incorporating mindfulness exercises, journaling, and making small adjustments to your routine, you can create a more supportive environment for yourself. Remember that these practices are not one-size-fits-all; experiment to find what resonates best with you. Taking these proactive steps can empower you to reclaim your mental well-being and navigate the entrepreneurial journey with renewed focus and resilience.

6

2.1 The Unique Mental Burdens of Entrepreneurship

Financial Stress and Unpredictability

Financial stress is one of the most significant and constant challenges for entrepreneurs. The unpredictability of running a business, coupled with the weight of financial responsibilities, can often feel overwhelming. It's not just about your own well-being—it's about the survival of your business, the people who rely on you, and the long-term stability you're trying to build. Let's explore some of the key aspects of financial stress that entrepreneurs commonly face.

The Pressure of Maintaining Cash Flow

One of the most persistent sources of financial stress is the ***pressure to maintain a steady cash flow***. As an entrepreneur, you are responsible for ensuring that your business has enough money coming in to cover its expenses, pay employees, and invest in growth. Cash flow is the lifeblood of any business, but when revenues fluctuate or unexpected costs arise, it can create a sense of constant financial insecurity. Whether it's slow sales, late payments from clients, or unforeseen expenses, these disruptions can leave you feeling like you're always on the edge, trying to juggle bills and payroll with no room for error. This pressure can take a toll not only on your business but also on your mental and emotional well-being.

Handling Personal and Business Expenses Simultaneously

Entrepreneurs often face the added challenge of ***managing personal and business expenses at the same time***. Unlike traditional employees who receive a stable paycheck, you may find yourself navigating the complexities of irregular income, which means you have to stretch resources to cover both business costs and personal expenses. This balancing act can be especially difficult when your business is going through lean times. It's easy for personal finances to become intertwined with the business, further complicating your situation. The stress of knowing that a bad month for your business can impact your personal life and vice versa can make you feel like you're constantly walking a financial tightrope.

Worrying About Employees' Livelihoods

On top of managing your own finances, the ***responsibility of your employees' livelihoods*** weighs heavily on your shoulders. Every paycheck you issue isn't just a business transaction—it's tied to the real lives and families of the people who work for you. This adds another layer of emotional pressure when cash flow becomes tight or the future of the business is uncertain. The thought of not being able to pay your team or having to make difficult decisions like cutting hours or laying off staff can cause immense anxiety. It's not just about the financial strain—it's the emotional toll of knowing that your decisions impact the people who have trusted you with their careers and well-being.

Financial stress and unpredictability are realities that almost every entrepreneur faces at some point. The pressure to maintain cash flow, manage personal and business expenses, and care for your employees can quickly become overwhelming. But recognizing these stressors is the first step in addressing them. By understanding the financial challenges you're up against, you can start to implement strategies, seek support, and make decisions that prioritise not only your business's success but also your mental health. Remember, you don't have to navigate this financial pressure alone—there are resources and people who can help you find solutions and regain stability.

The Culture of Hustle and Overwork

In today's entrepreneurial world, there's a pervasive culture that glorifies the hustle—where working long hours and pushing yourself to the limit are seen as badges of honour. The belief that success comes only through relentless grind has been romanticised, often at the expense of mental and physical health. This culture of overwork can be toxic, trapping entrepreneurs in a cycle of exhaustion, guilt, and burnout. Let's take a closer look at the impact of this mentality.

The Glorification of Working Long Hours

One of the key aspects of hustle culture is the ***glorification of long hours***. As an entrepreneur, it's easy to buy into the idea that working around the clock is a necessary part of success. Society often celebrates those who "hustle" nonstop, as if putting in more hours automatically leads to greater achievement. You may feel pressure to be the first one in and the last one out, constantly pushing yourself, as though every spare moment should be spent working. But this relentless pursuit of productivity can take a serious toll on your mental and physical health. Working excessively not only leads to burnout, but it can also diminish your creativity and decision-making ability—the very qualities that helped you build your business in the first place.

Guilt Around Taking Breaks or Resting

This culture of hustle often creates a sense of ***guilt around taking breaks or resting***. As an entrepreneur, you might feel that every minute you're not working is a minute lost—an opportunity missed to grow your business. Even when you know you're exhausted or mentally drained, taking time off can feel like failure. The constant pressure to be "on" and available can leave you feeling guilty when you take a day off, spend time with family, or even just step away from your desk for an hour. This guilt can be overwhelming, making it difficult to find balance and pushing you further into the cycle of overwork. However, the reality is that rest is crucial to your long-term success—both personally and professionally. Without adequate breaks, you risk running yourself into the ground, which ultimately hinders your ability to lead and innovate.

The Belief That Constant Activity Equals Success

At the heart of hustle culture is the ***belief that constant activity equals success***. There's an underlying notion that the busier you are, the more successful you'll become. But busyness doesn't always translate to progress, and constant activity can mask inefficiency or distract you from your true goals. It's easy to fall into the trap of measuring your worth by how full your calendar is or how many hours you've clocked, rather than the quality of the work you're doing or the strategic decisions you're making. True success isn't about being in perpetual motion—it's about knowing when to focus, when to step back, and when to recharge so that you can bring your best self to the work that truly matters.

The culture of hustle and overwork can be incredibly harmful, leading to burnout, frustration, and a distorted view of what success really looks like. Recognizing the glorification of long hours, the guilt around resting, and the myth that constant activity equals progress is essential for breaking free from this toxic mindset. Taking care of yourself—both mentally and physically—should be seen as part of your entrepreneurial success, not a hindrance to it. Finding a balance between hard work and rest is not only healthier but also more sustainable in the long run.

Fear of Failure and Its Psychological Effects

For many entrepreneurs, the ***fear of failure*** runs deep, often becoming a driving force behind every decision. While this fear can sometimes fuel ambition and push you to succeed, it can also have significant psychological effects, leaving you feeling trapped and overwhelmed. The connection between your personal identity and your business performance, combined with the pressure to meet public expectations, can create an emotional burden that's hard to shake.

The Personal Connection Between Self-Worth and Business Performance

As an entrepreneur, it's common to ***tie your self-worth directly to your business performance***. Your business is more than just a job—it's often a reflection of your vision, creativity, and hard work. When things are going well, it can feel like a validation of who you are. But when your business faces challenges, that sense of self-worth can quickly diminish. The line between personal failure and business failure becomes blurred, leading to feelings of inadequacy or shame when things don't go as planned. This emotional weight makes every setback feel personal, amplifying the fear that you're not enough, and that failure in business means failure as a person.

How Fear of Failure Leads to Procrastination

One of the ways this fear manifests is through ***procrastination***. The anxiety around potentially failing can cause you to delay making decisions or taking action, even when you know it's necessary. You might avoid important tasks or push off big decisions because the risk of failure feels too high to face. Instead of diving in, you find yourself stuck in a cycle of overthinking, hesitating, or distracting yourself with less critical tasks. Procrastination becomes a way to avoid the discomfort of uncertainty, but ultimately, it stalls progress and creates even more stress. The fear of failure doesn't just prevent action—it creates a self-fulfilling prophecy, where the avoidance of risk leads to missed opportunities and stagnation.

Handling Public Perceptions of Business Setbacks

In addition to the internal struggles, there's also the external pressure of ***public perceptions*** when your business faces setbacks. The fear of how others will view your failure can weigh heavily on your mind. Whether it's investors, customers, employees, or even friends and family, the concern over disappointing others or being seen as unsuccessful can add to the emotional burden. The entrepreneurial journey is often under a spotlight, and when things go wrong, it can feel like the world is watching. This fear of public judgment can make it even harder to cope with setbacks, as the pressure to maintain an image of success becomes overwhelming. Navigating these perceptions requires resilience and a reminder that setbacks are a natural part of business—and that they do not define your worth or long-term potential.

2.1 THE UNIQUE MENTAL BURDENS OF ENTREPRENEURSHIP

The *fear of failure* is a powerful force, but it doesn't have to control your entrepreneurial journey. By recognizing how deeply personal this fear can feel, understanding its role in procrastination, and learning to navigate public perceptions, you can begin to re-frame your relationship with failure. It's important to remember that failure is not the opposite of success—it's a part of the process. Facing it head-on, with self-compassion and resilience, is key to growing both as a business owner and as a person.

2.2 How Entrepreneurship Impacts Personal Relationships

Strain on Family and Romantic Relationships

Running a business often demands your time, energy, and focus—but when these demands take over, they can start to affect your personal life in significant ways. The ***strain on family and romantic relationships*** is a common challenge many entrepreneurs face, as the pressures of work spill over into personal time. The emotional toll of balancing a business with maintaining meaningful connections can lead to feelings of guilt, resentment, and disconnection from the people who matter most.

Being Emotionally Unavailable Due to Work Stress

One of the most difficult consequences of entrepreneurship is becoming ***emotionally unavailable*** to your loved ones. When you're consumed by work stress, it's easy to find yourself mentally checked out, even when you're physically present. You might come home at the end of a long day only to find that you're too exhausted or preoccupied to engage in meaningful conversations or share quality time. This emotional distance can create a disconnect in your relationships, leaving your partner, family, or friends feeling like they are no longer a priority. Over time, this can erode the emotional bond you share, as work stress dominates your thoughts and leaves little room for the needs of your personal life.

Resentment from Loved Ones Over Time Spent Working

Another challenge that often arises is ***resentment from loved ones*** over the amount of time you spend working. While you may be working long hours out of necessity, your family or partner may begin to feel neglected or frustrated. They may struggle to understand why you can't step away from your business to be more present in their lives. This resentment can build over time, leading to tension and conflict within the relationship. Your loved ones might feel as though they are competing with your business for your attention, and this can create feelings of hurt, anger, or abandonment. Balancing these competing demands—your business and your personal life—can feel impossible at times, but acknowledging the strain is the first step toward finding a solution.

Managing Feelings of Guilt Over Neglecting Personal Relationships

For entrepreneurs, the constant pull between work and personal life often leads to ***feelings of guilt***. You might recognize that you've been neglecting your relationships, but feel trapped by the demands of your business. The guilt can weigh heavily, especially when you miss important family events, cancel plans with friends, or fail to be present for your partner when they need you. This guilt can create a vicious cycle: the more you work to support your business, the more disconnected you feel from your loved ones, and the more guilt you carry as a result. Over time, this guilt can deepen feelings of isolation and strain your emotional well-being.

Managing these challenges requires open communication, boundaries, and a commitment to balancing the needs of both your business and your personal relationships. It's important to be honest with your loved ones about the pressures you're facing, while also making time to nurture those relationships. Small, intentional moments of connection can help rebuild the bond, and setting clearer boundaries around work time can ensure that you're not always on the clock. Remember that success in business doesn't have to come at the cost of your most important relationships—finding that balance is essential for your happiness and fulfillment in the long run.

Difficulty Maintaining Friendships

As an entrepreneur, maintaining friendships can often become a challenge, especially as your time and energy are consumed by the demands of running a business. The social connections that once brought joy and support may start to feel distant, strained, or even irrelevant as your focus shifts to your work. This disconnection can lead to feelings of loneliness, isolation, and a growing sense of being misunderstood, particularly by friends who don't share the entrepreneurial journey.

Losing Touch with Old Friends Due to Time Constraints

One of the most common issues is simply ***losing touch with old friends***. The intense time constraints of entrepreneurship often mean that social engagements fall to the bottom of the priority list. While you may have once had time for regular meetups, phone calls, or casual hangouts, these moments become rarer as your business requires more attention. Before long, weeks and months pass without meaningful contact, and friendships that once felt close start to fade away. This isn't always intentional, but the constant demands of running a business can leave little time for maintaining personal connections, creating an emotional gap between you and your friends.

Feeling Misunderstood by Non-Entrepreneurial Friends

Even when you do make time for friends, it can be difficult to relate to those who aren't familiar with the entrepreneurial world. You may begin ***feeling misunderstood by non-entrepreneurial friends***, who might not fully grasp the pressures, sacrifices, or emotional toll that come with running a business. Conversations about long hours, financial stress, or the constant pressure to succeed may fall flat or be met with well-meaning but misplaced advice. This disconnect can leave you feeling like your friends don't really understand what you're going through, creating a sense of emotional distance even when you're spending time together. It's not that they don't care, but the nature of entrepreneurship is difficult to fully comprehend for those who haven't experienced it firsthand.

The Loneliness of Not Sharing Struggles with Anyone

Perhaps the most profound challenge is the ***loneliness of not sharing your struggles with anyone***. Many entrepreneurs feel the need to put on a brave face, to project confidence and optimism, even when things are tough. This can lead to a reluctance to open up about your struggles, whether they're related to your business, finances, or mental health. Without a trusted confidant to share the weight of these challenges, you may feel like you're carrying the burden alone. The loneliness of entrepreneurship is compounded by the fact that, while you may be surrounded by people—clients, employees, even friends—you might not feel truly understood or supported in your personal journey.

Maintaining friendships as an entrepreneur requires effort and intent. It's important to recognize the value of these relationships and make space for them, even in the midst of a busy schedule. Seeking out connections with other entrepreneurs can also be incredibly helpful, as they will better understand the highs and lows you're experiencing. Remember, friendships are not just about support during the good times—they're about having people who can walk alongside you through the challenges. Taking the time to nurture these bonds can provide the connection and understanding that help combat the loneliness that so often comes with entrepreneurship.

Building a Support System Within the Business Community

As an entrepreneur, it's easy to feel like you're navigating uncharted waters alone. The unique challenges and pressures of building and growing a business often require a level of understanding that only fellow entrepreneurs can offer. That's why **building a support system within the business community** can be a game-changer—not just for your business, but for your mental and emotional well-being. Surrounding yourself with like-minded individuals who share your experiences can provide invaluable support, guidance, and camaraderie.

Finding Entrepreneurial Peers Who Understand the Journey

One of the most significant benefits of connecting with ***entrepreneurial peers*** is finding people who truly understand the highs and lows of the journey. Unlike non-entrepreneurial friends or family, these peers have faced similar struggles—whether it's the stress of managing cash flow, the emotional toll of constant decision-making, or the pressure to succeed despite setbacks. By seeking out relationships with fellow entrepreneurs, you create a space where you can share your experiences, ask for advice, and simply be understood without needing to explain yourself. These connections can help alleviate the isolation that often comes with entrepreneurship, providing you with a network of people who know exactly what you're going through.

Benefits of Joining Business Networks and Mastermind Groups

One of the best ways to build these connections is by ***joining business networks or mastermind groups***. Business networks offer opportunities to meet like-minded individuals, exchange ideas, and form meaningful relationships with people who can provide both practical advice and emotional support. Mastermind groups, in particular, are focused on helping members grow their businesses through regular meetings, problem-solving sessions, and goal-setting discussions. These groups not only give you access to valuable insights from fellow entrepreneurs but also hold you accountable in ways that can drive personal and business growth. More than just networking, these environments foster deep relationships where you can openly discuss challenges and celebrate successes with people who are walking a similar path.

2.2 HOW ENTREPRENEURSHIP IMPACTS PERSONAL RELATIONSHIPS

How Collaboration Over Competition Can Improve Well-Being

There's often a misconception in the business world that ***competition*** is the only way to succeed. But in reality, focusing on ***collaboration over competition*** can lead to better results and improved well-being. Collaborating with fellow entrepreneurs fosters a sense of community and support, rather than isolation and rivalry. When you view other business owners as potential collaborators rather than competitors, you open up opportunities for sharing resources, knowledge, and even customers. This mindset shift can reduce the stress of feeling like you're constantly up against others and instead create a supportive network where everyone benefits. By building genuine, collaborative relationships, you also gain a sense of belonging, which can significantly boost your emotional health and contribute to your overall success.

Incorporating a strong support system within the business community can be one of the most rewarding investments you make—not just for your business but for your personal well-being. Whether through finding entrepreneurial peers, joining networks or mastermind groups, or fostering collaboration, these connections can help you manage the unique challenges of entrepreneurship. It's not just about growing your business; it's about creating a network of support where you can thrive both personally and professionally.

8

2.3 The Biological and Psychological Aspects of Depression

The Role of Brain Chemistry in Depression

When it comes to depression, it's not just external stressors or life circumstances that play a role—*your brain chemistry is deeply involved* as well. Understanding the biological side of depression can help demystify some of the emotional and mental challenges you face. While the entrepreneurial journey is full of unique stresses, the way your brain responds to these pressures on a chemical level can greatly impact your mood, mental health, and overall well-being. Let's explore how brain chemistry influences depression and what you can do to support a healthier mental state.

2.3 THE BIOLOGICAL AND PSYCHOLOGICAL ASPECTS OF DEPRESSION

How Serotonin and Dopamine Levels Affect Mood

Two key neurotransmitters, **serotonin** and **dopamine**, play a significant role in regulating your mood. Serotonin is often referred to as the "feel-good" chemical, as it helps regulate mood, sleep, and appetite, while also contributing to feelings of well-being and happiness. Low levels of serotonin are commonly linked to feelings of sadness, anxiety, and depression. Dopamine, on the other hand, is known as the "reward" chemical and is crucial for motivation, pleasure, and focus. When dopamine levels are low, it can lead to a lack of enthusiasm, difficulty experiencing pleasure, and feelings of apathy. Both serotonin and dopamine can be depleted by chronic stress, lack of sleep, or poor diet—all common challenges in the life of an entrepreneur. Understanding how these neurotransmitters influence your mood can help you identify ways to restore balance and improve your mental health.

Understanding How Stress Affects Brain Function

Chronic stress is one of the most significant contributors to depression, and it has a direct impact on how your brain functions. Prolonged stress triggers the release of **cortisol**, a hormone designed to help you handle short-term stress. However, when cortisol levels remain elevated over long periods, it can disrupt brain function, impair memory, and even shrink the prefrontal cortex—the part of the brain responsible for decision-making and emotional regulation. This makes it harder to cope with everyday challenges, leading to feelings of pressure and exacerbating symptoms of depression. Entrepreneurs often live in a state of chronic stress due to the constant demands of running a business, making it crucial to find ways to manage stress effectively and protect your brain health.

The Impact of Sleep and Diet on Mental Health

Your *sleep* and *diet* have a profound impact on your brain chemistry and overall mental health. Sleep is essential for the brain's ability to regulate mood and process emotions. When you're sleep-deprived, your brain struggles to produce enough serotonin and dopamine, leading to irritability, mood swings, and worsened symptoms of depression. Sleep also allows your brain to detoxify and recover from the stresses of the day, so consistently poor sleep can worsen your mental health over time.

Similarly, *diet* plays a vital role in supporting brain function and mood regulation. The brain requires a steady supply of nutrients—like omega-3 fatty acids, B vitamins, and amino acids—to produce neurotransmitters that regulate your mood. A diet high in processed foods and low in these essential nutrients can contribute to chemical imbalances in the brain, exacerbating feelings of depression. Conversely, a well-balanced diet rich in whole foods can support healthier brain function, improve mood, and even help manage stress more effectively.

By understanding the role of **brain chemistry** in depression, you can take a more holistic approach to managing your mental health. Supporting serotonin and dopamine levels, managing stress, and taking care of your sleep and diet are all steps that can help restore balance to your brain and improve your overall mood. While entrepreneurship may bring many challenges, paying attention to your brain's needs can empower you to take better care of your mental health as you navigate the ups and downs of the journey.

Environmental Factors Contributing to Depression

While depression is often associated with internal emotional and mental struggles, the environment around you plays a significant role in shaping your mental health as well. As an entrepreneur, your workspace, the people you interact with (or don't interact with), and the pressures of constant stress can all contribute to feelings of depression. By understanding how these ***environmental factors*** impact your well-being, you can take proactive steps to create a healthier, more supportive space for yourself.

The Effect of Isolation from Peers or Colleagues

Entrepreneurship can be a lonely journey, and ***isolation from peers or colleagues*** is a common issue. Many entrepreneurs work independently or with small teams, spending long hours disconnected from social interactions that are vital for maintaining a sense of community and support. Without regular opportunities to share ideas, vent frustrations, or simply connect on a human level, you can start to feel isolated, which can deepen feelings of loneliness and depression. Humans are social creatures, and even if you're an introvert, the lack of meaningful connection with others can negatively impact your mental health. Finding ways to engage with a community of like-minded peers, either through networking, co-working spaces, or mastermind groups, can help counteract this isolation and provide much-needed emotional support.

How Constant Stress Increases Cortisol Levels

Entrepreneurs often live in a state of **constant stress**, juggling multiple responsibilities and dealing with the uncertainties that come with running a business. This unrelenting stress can lead to chronically elevated levels of **cortisol**, the body's primary stress hormone. While cortisol is useful in short bursts to help you respond to immediate threats or challenges, prolonged exposure to high cortisol levels has serious negative effects on both your body and mind. Elevated cortisol can disrupt sleep, impair cognitive function, and lead to a constant state of tension or anxiety. Over time, this chronic stress response can contribute to depression, as your brain becomes less able to regulate mood and emotions effectively. Managing stress through mindfulness, relaxation techniques, or even taking regular breaks is essential for lowering cortisol levels and protecting your mental health.

The Importance of Workspace Design and Location on Mood

Your **workspace** plays a surprisingly important role in shaping your mood and productivity. A cluttered, poorly lit, or uncomfortable workspace can contribute to feelings of pressure, stress, and even depression. In contrast, a well-designed, organized space can help create a sense of calm and focus. Elements like natural light, greenery, ergonomic furniture, and even the colours you surround yourself with can influence your emotional state. For instance, natural light boosts serotonin levels, helping to improve mood, while plants can reduce stress and increase feelings of well-being. Additionally, the **location** of your workspace matters—working in a noisy or distracting environment, or feeling confined to a small, uninspiring space, can lead to irritability and frustration. Designing a workspace that is both functional and pleasant can have a positive impact on your mental health, making it easier to focus, manage stress, and maintain a healthier emotional state.

By addressing these ***environmental factors***, you can create a more supportive and balanced environment that promotes better mental health. Whether it's seeking out social connections, managing stress, or improving your workspace, these changes can help alleviate some of the external pressures that contribute to depression. In doing so, you'll be better equipped to handle the challenges of entrepreneurship while protecting your well-being.

Genetic Predispositions to Mental Health Challenges

While environmental factors and life circumstances play a significant role in shaping mental health, ***genetic predispositions*** can also influence your susceptibility to depression and anxiety. Recognizing the role of genetics in mental health can help you better understand your emotional landscape and take proactive steps to manage any underlying tendencies. If mental health challenges run in your family, you may be more vulnerable to these struggles, even if they aren't directly linked to external stressors like entrepreneurship.

Recognizing Family Histories of Depression or Anxiety

One of the first steps in understanding genetic predispositions is ***recognizing family histories of depression or anxiety***. If you have close relatives—parents, siblings, or grandparents—who have experienced depression, anxiety, or other mental health disorders, you may be at an increased risk of developing similar conditions. Mental health conditions often have a hereditary component, meaning that they can be passed down through generations. Being aware of your family's mental health history can help you stay vigilant about your own well-being and recognize early signs of depression or anxiety before they escalate.

How Genetics Can Interact with Life Circumstances

While genetics may increase your likelihood of experiencing mental health challenges, they often ***interact with life circumstances*** in complex ways. For example, an individual with a genetic predisposition to depression may only experience symptoms when triggered by significant stressors, such as financial strain, work pressures, or personal loss. In other words, genetics alone do not determine your mental health—environmental factors, lifestyle, and coping mechanisms also play a crucial role. Entrepreneurs, who frequently face high levels of stress, may find that their genetic predispositions are activated during particularly challenging times. This interaction between genetics and life stressors makes it essential to manage external pressures while being mindful of your mental health.

Knowing When Depression May Be Beyond Situational Triggers

While external factors like stress, isolation, or financial pressure can certainly contribute to feelings of depression, there may come a point when ***depression is beyond situational triggers***. If you notice that depressive symptoms persist even when life circumstances improve—or that the intensity of your depression seems disproportionate to your current challenges—it may indicate that your depression is more deeply rooted in genetics. This kind of depression may not respond as easily to situational changes, such as reducing stress or improving work-life balance, and might require professional intervention, such as therapy or medication. Recognizing when your depression goes beyond situational triggers can be a turning point in seeking the appropriate treatment and understanding that it may be a deeper, biologically-based condition.

Acknowledging that ***genetic predispositions*** can play a role in your mental health is empowering. It allows you to be more aware of your emotional tendencies and take proactive steps to manage them. Whether your depression or anxiety is triggered by external circumstances or is more deeply rooted in your genetic makeup, being mindful of these influences can help you make informed decisions about seeking treatment and finding effective coping strategies. Understanding that genetics might be a factor doesn't mean you're destined to struggle—it means you have the knowledge to manage your mental health more effectively, no matter where the challenges originate.

9

3.1 Building a Healthy Work-Life Balance

Setting Clear Boundaries Between Work and Personal Life

As an entrepreneur, it can be incredibly challenging to separate your work life from your personal life. With the constant demands of running a business, it's easy for the lines to blur, leading to burnout and mental exhaustion. However, **setting clear boundaries** is crucial for maintaining your well-being, preserving your personal relationships, and ensuring long-term success. Here are a few strategies that can help you create and maintain those boundaries.

Scheduling Time Off and Sticking to It

One of the most important things you can do for yourself is **scheduling time off**—and actually sticking to it. This can be harder than it sounds, especially when you're used to being "on" all the time. But just as you would schedule a meeting or a project deadline, it's important to treat your personal time with the same level of commitment. Block out specific times during the week when you'll disconnect from work, whether it's evenings, weekends, or entire days. Use this time to recharge, connect with loved ones, or simply relax without the pressures of work looming over you. By consistently honouring these breaks, you'll protect your mental health and prevent burnout, making you more productive when you return to your tasks.

Creating a Dedicated Workspace at Home or in an Office

When working from home or managing a remote team, it's easy to feel like you're always at work. To combat this, ***creating a dedicated workspace*** can help establish a clear separation between your professional and personal life. Whether it's a specific room in your house or a desk in a quiet corner, having a designated space for work can help mentally signal when it's time to focus on business and when it's time to relax. If possible, keeping your workspace separate from where you unwind or sleep can make it easier to switch off at the end of the day. This boundary between physical spaces can reduce stress and create a healthier balance between work and home life. If you have the option, working from a dedicated office or co-working space can provide even more structure, giving you a clear distinction between "work mode" and "home mode."

Learning to Say No to Non-Critical Tasks

Entrepreneurs often feel the need to take on everything themselves, but learning to **say no to non-critical tasks** is a vital part of maintaining boundaries. It's easy to get caught up in the idea that every task is important, but not everything demands your immediate attention. Prioritise the tasks that are essential to your business's growth and delegate or defer the ones that aren't. Saying no doesn't mean you're neglecting your business; it means you're protecting your time and energy for the things that truly matter. Being selective about what you take on can help you avoid pressure and create more room in your schedule for personal time and self-care.

Establishing clear boundaries between work and personal life is a crucial step in maintaining both your mental health and your business's success. By **scheduling time off**, **creating a dedicated workspace**, and **learning to say no**, you can build a healthier, more sustainable balance. These boundaries not only protect your well-being but also ensure that when you're working, you're focused, energised, and at your best.

Delegating and Outsourcing Tasks

As an entrepreneur, you may feel the pressure to handle every aspect of your business yourself, but this mindset can quickly lead to burnout and inefficiency. One of the most powerful ways to protect your mental health and ensure the long-term success of your business is through effective **delegation and outsourcing**. Learning how to strategically hand off tasks, hire the right team, and leverage technology can lighten your load and give you more time to focus on the most important aspects of your work.

Understanding What You Don't Have to Do Yourself

The first step in delegating is recognizing that ***you don't have to do everything yourself***. As a business owner, your time and energy are valuable resources, and they should be reserved for tasks that only you can do—such as setting the vision for your company or making high-level decisions. Everything else, from administrative tasks to marketing efforts, can likely be handled by someone else. Start by identifying which tasks drain your time and energy but aren't critical to your role as a leader. By letting go of control over these non-essential duties, you free up mental space to focus on the bigger picture, where your expertise and creativity are most needed.

How to Hire the Right Team Members to Lighten Your Load

Delegation works best when you have the right people in place to support you. **Hiring the right team members** is essential for lightening your load and ensuring that tasks are completed effectively. Look for individuals whose skills complement your own and who are capable of taking ownership of their responsibilities. Whether it's an administrative assistant, a marketing manager, or an operations lead, each team member should be empowered to manage their area with minimal oversight from you. Clear communication, trust, and providing the necessary tools and training are key to successful delegation. When you build a capable team, you not only reduce your own workload but also create a stronger, more resilient business.

Investing in your team pays off in the long run, as it allows you to step back from day-to-day operations and focus on scaling your business.

Leveraging Technology and Tools to Automate Tasks

In addition to hiring a strong team, **leveraging technology and tools** can help you automate many of the routine tasks that take up time. There are countless platforms available that can streamline everything from accounting and invoicing to customer relationship management (CRM) and email marketing. By automating repetitive tasks, you reduce the mental and physical toll of managing every small detail. For example, using scheduling software can automate meetings and reminders, while tools like project management platforms can keep your team on track without your constant involvement. These technologies allow you to stay organised, improve efficiency, and spend less time on administrative work. The key is to choose the right tools that fit your business needs and integrate them into your workflow.

Learning to **delegate** and **outsource** is a critical skill for entrepreneurs. By recognizing what you don't have to do yourself, building a team that can take on important responsibilities, and automating tasks through technology, you can reclaim your time and mental energy. This not only helps your business run more smoothly but also allows you to focus on what you do best while maintaining a healthier work-life balance.

Prioritising Self-Care Without Guilt

Entrepreneurs often put their businesses first, neglecting their own well-being in the process. However, **prioritising self-care** is essential for both personal health and business success. Taking care of yourself not only boosts your mental and physical health but also enables you to perform better as a leader. The challenge is learning to prioritise self-care without feeling guilty about stepping away from work. Here are a few strategies for achieving that balance.

Setting Aside Time for Hobbies and Relaxation

One of the most effective ways to maintain your mental health is by **setting aside time for hobbies and relaxation**. While it can feel difficult to justify time away from work, especially when you're deeply invested in your business, taking breaks to engage in activities you enjoy is crucial for recharging your mind and spirit. Whether it's reading, painting, gardening, or simply spending time with loved ones, these moments allow you to decompress and step back from the demands of running a business. Scheduling this time as you would a meeting ensures that you make room for it, helping you strike a balance between productivity and personal fulfillment. Remember, downtime isn't wasted time—it's essential for sustaining long-term focus and energy.

Why Exercise and Movement Are Key to Mental Health

Exercise and movement are some of the most powerful tools for maintaining mental health. Physical activity releases endorphins, which improve mood and reduce stress, while also helping you maintain your energy levels throughout the day. Whether it's a daily walk, yoga session, or more intense exercise like running or weightlifting, regular movement helps clear your mind and enhances your emotional resilience. Exercise is also linked to better sleep, improved focus, and a stronger ability to cope with the challenges of entrepreneurship. Incorporating movement into your daily routine doesn't have to be time-consuming—even a 10-15 minute workout or stretching session can make a significant difference in how you feel. It's an investment in your mental health that will pay off in both your personal life and your business.

Balancing Business Success with Personal Well-Being

Balancing ***business success with personal well-being*** requires you to shift your mindset from one of constant hustle to one of sustainable productivity. Success isn't about how many hours you put in—it's about the quality of those hours and how effectively you manage your time and energy. By taking care of your personal well-being, you're not only improving your mental health but also enhancing your ability to make sound decisions, lead with clarity, and manage stress. It's important to remind yourself that you don't need to sacrifice your health for the sake of your business. Finding a rhythm that allows you to prioritise both your personal needs and your professional goals will lead to better outcomes in the long run.

Prioritising self-care without guilt is about recognizing that your well-being is just as important as your business. By **setting aside time for hobbies**, embracing **exercise as a tool for mental health**, and **balancing success with personal care**, you can create a healthier, more sustainable approach to both work and life. You'll find that taking care of yourself not only benefits you but also makes you a more effective, focused, and resilient entrepreneur.

10

3.2 Managing Stress through Daily Habits

The Power of Routine in Reducing Anxiety

In the unpredictable world of entrepreneurship, having a consistent routine can provide much-needed stability and help reduce anxiety. Establishing daily rhythms allows you to create a sense of control over your time, which is especially important when business demands can often feel overwhelming. A well-structured routine not only improves your productivity but also helps protect your mental health by reducing stress and uncertainty. Here's how the power of routine can work for you.

Structuring Your Day with Regular Work Hours

One of the most effective ways to reduce anxiety is by ***structuring your day with regular work hours***. While flexibility can be a benefit of entrepreneurship, it's easy for that flexibility to turn into a lack of boundaries—where work bleeds into all hours of the day and night. Setting clear, consistent work hours helps you compartmentalise your time, ensuring that you're productive during specific periods and able to relax outside of those hours. This structure creates a healthy separation between your professional and personal life, reducing the anxiety that comes with feeling like you're always working or "on call." Stick to a routine where you start and end your workday at the same time whenever possible, helping your brain shift into work mode and then into relaxation mode at predictable intervals.

Incorporating Time for Reflection, Exercise, and Leisure

A routine isn't just about work—it's also about making intentional time for ***reflection, exercise, and leisure***. These activities play a crucial role in maintaining mental clarity and reducing stress. Incorporating daily reflection, whether through journaling, meditation or simply taking a few quiet moments to think, helps you process your thoughts and emotions, making it easier to navigate challenges with a clearer mindset. ***Exercise***, as mentioned earlier, is key to reducing anxiety by releasing endorphins and helping you manage stress. Lastly, don't overlook the importance of ***leisure***—whether that's spending time on hobbies, connecting with friends, or relaxing with a book. Making time for these activities within your **daily routine** ensures you're caring for both your mind and body, creating balance in your life that wards off burnout and anxiety.

Limiting Time Spent on Non-Essential Tasks Like Social Media

While some tasks are necessary for running a business, others—like *social media* and other distractions—can easily consume more time than they're worth, contributing to unnecessary stress and anxiety. One of the most powerful ways to reduce anxiety is by *limiting time spent on non-essential tasks*. Social media, in particular, can be a major drain on your energy, often leading to comparison, information overload, or distraction. Set specific times during the day to check emails or social media, rather than constantly switching between work and distractions. By limiting these activities, you'll find more time to focus on what truly matters and reduce the mental clutter that can lead to anxiety.

Building a *routine* is one of the simplest yet most powerful ways to reduce anxiety and create a sense of balance in your life. By *structuring your day with regular work hours*, ensuring time for *reflection, exercise, and leisure*, and *limiting non-essential tasks*, you can take control of your time and mental space. A well-balanced routine not only helps you manage your business more effectively but also protects your mental health, allowing you to thrive both personally and professionally.

Practicing Mindfulness and Relaxation Techniques

In the fast-paced world of entrepreneurship, finding ways to manage stress and maintain mental clarity is essential. One of the most effective ways to achieve this is through *mindfulness and relaxation techniques*. These practices help you stay grounded, reduce stress, and improve your emotional resilience, even during the busiest or most challenging times. By incorporating mindfulness into your daily routine, you can cultivate a sense of calm and focus that benefits both your well-being and your work.

Meditation or Breathing Exercises for Stress Relief

One of the simplest and most accessible mindfulness practices is ***meditation*** or ***breathing exercises***. Both techniques are powerful tools for managing stress and anxiety. Meditation allows you to clear your mind and focus on the present moment, helping you break the cycle of overthinking or worrying about the future. You can start with just a few minutes each day, sitting quietly and focusing on your breath or a calming mantra. Breathing exercises, such as ***deep belly breathing*** or the ***4-7-8 breathing technique***, can quickly reduce feelings of stress by activating the body's relaxation response. These exercises slow down your heart rate and reduce tension, making them an excellent way to regain focus and calm during a hectic day. Incorporating just a few minutes of meditation or deep breathing into your routine can provide significant relief from daily stressors.

Progressive Muscle Relaxation for Tension Release

Another highly effective technique for stress management is ***progressive muscle relaxation (PMR)***. This practice involves systematically tensing and then releasing each muscle group in your body, helping you become more aware of where you're holding tension and allowing you to consciously release it.

Start by focusing on your feet, tensing the muscles for a few seconds, then relaxing them completely. Gradually work your way up through your body—legs, abdomen, shoulders, arms, and finally, your face. By the end of the exercise, you'll likely feel more relaxed and less tense. PMR is particularly useful for people who carry physical stress in their bodies, and it can be a quick, effective way to release built-up tension at the end of a long day or during a stressful moment.

How to Integrate Small Mindfulness Breaks into the Workday

Incorporating mindfulness doesn't have to take up large chunks of your time. In fact, **small mindfulness breaks** throughout the workday can have a huge impact on reducing stress and boosting productivity. These breaks can be as simple as taking a few deep breaths before starting a new task, doing a quick body scan to check in with how you're feeling, or stepping outside for a few minutes of fresh air and a mental reset. Even short mindfulness moments, like sipping your coffee mindfully by focusing on the aroma, temperature, and taste, can help you stay present and grounded. Set reminders on your phone or calendar to pause briefly throughout the day to check in with yourself. These micro-breaks allow you to recharge mentally and emotionally, ensuring that you remain calm and focused no matter how busy your day gets.

Mindfulness and relaxation techniques are invaluable tools for entrepreneurs looking to reduce stress and maintain a sense of balance. By incorporating *meditation or breathing exercises*, practicing *progressive muscle relaxation*, and integrating *small mindfulness breaks* into your workday, you can manage stress more effectively and improve your overall well-being. These simple, accessible practices can make a profound difference in your mental health, helping you stay centered and focused amid the demands of entrepreneurship.

Creating a Healthy Sleep Environment

Sleep is one of the most essential pillars of mental and physical health, yet it's often the first thing entrepreneurs sacrifice during busy periods. However, *creating a healthy sleep environment* and maintaining good sleep hygiene can dramatically improve your rest quality, helping you stay sharp, focused, and resilient. Getting enough restorative sleep is key to managing stress and avoiding burnout, so here's how to make sleep a priority, even when your schedule feels overwhelming.

Maintaining Consistent Sleep Schedules Even During Busy Periods

One of the most important steps in improving sleep is *maintaining a consistent sleep schedule*. Entrepreneurs often work late into the night or wake up early, leading to irregular sleep patterns that can disrupt the body's **natural circadian rhythm.** Even during the busiest times, it's crucial to go to bed and wake up at the same time each day. Consistency helps regulate your internal clock, making it easier to fall asleep and wake up naturally. Sticking to a routine, even on weekends, can improve the overall quality of your sleep, ensuring you're rested and ready to tackle the day's challenges with clarity and energy.

Avoiding Work-Related Distractions Before Bed

It's tempting to check emails or think through tomorrow's to-do list just before bed, but **work-related distractions** can make it much harder to wind down and fall asleep. Engaging in work-related activities before bed stimulates the brain, making it difficult to relax and shut off your mind. Set a cutoff time for work-related tasks—ideally at least an hour before bed—and use this time to transition into relaxation mode. Avoid checking your phone, laptop, or any work materials in the lead-up to sleep. Instead, focus on calming activities such as reading, gentle stretching, or practicing relaxation techniques. Creating a boundary between work and bedtime helps your mind shift into a more peaceful state, which leads to better sleep.

Using Sleep Hygiene Techniques to Improve Rest Quality

Sleep hygiene refers to the habits and practices that promote consistent, restful sleep. By adopting some simple sleep hygiene techniques, you can improve the quality of your rest. Start by creating a sleep-friendly environment—keep your bedroom cool, quiet, and dark to support relaxation. Investing in comfortable bedding, blackout curtains, or white noise machines can make a big difference. Limit exposure to screens at least an hour before bed, as the blue light from devices can interfere with your body's production of melatonin, the hormone that regulates sleep. Additionally, consider establishing a relaxing pre-sleep routine, such as taking a warm bath, practicing meditation, or engaging in deep breathing exercises to signal to your body that it's time to wind down. Avoid caffeine and heavy meals late in the day, as these can disrupt your sleep cycle.

Creating a ***healthy sleep environment*** is crucial for maintaining the energy and focus needed to run a business successfully. By ***maintaining a consistent sleep schedule***, ***avoiding work-related distractions before bed***, and implementing ***sleep hygiene techniques***, you can ensure that you're getting the restorative sleep your body and mind need. Prioritising sleep isn't just about feeling well-rested—it's about optimising your overall well-being and setting yourself up for sustainable success in both business and life.

11

3.3 Professional Resources for Mental Health Support

Therapy and Counseling Options for Entrepreneurs

Running a business comes with unique challenges and stresses that can take a toll on your mental health. Whether it's managing constant decision-making, financial pressures, or the isolation of entrepreneurship, having a support system is essential. ***Therapy and counseling*** offer valuable tools for managing these mental health challenges, providing a space to work through emotions, develop coping strategies, and maintain mental clarity. Here's how therapy can help, particularly for entrepreneurs, and the options available for busy professionals.

The Benefits of Talking to a Professional Who Understands Business Pressures

One of the greatest benefits of therapy for entrepreneurs is the opportunity to **talk to a professional who understands the unique pressures** that come with running a business. A therapist experienced in working with business owners can help you navigate stress, burnout, and the emotional ups and downs that often accompany entrepreneurship. They can offer perspective on how your mental health is affecting your work performance, relationships, and personal life. Having someone who understands the complexities of entrepreneurship means you won't have to explain every challenge in great detail—they'll already know the pressures of financial responsibility, managing teams, and long hours. This makes the therapeutic process more efficient and relevant to your specific needs, allowing you to focus on finding solutions and building resilience.

Cognitive-behavioural Therapy (CBT) for Managing Negative Thoughts

Cognitive-behavioural therapy (CBT) is a widely-used therapeutic approach that is particularly effective for entrepreneurs struggling with stress, anxiety, or depression. CBT helps you identify and challenge **negative thought patterns** that can fuel feelings of pressure, self-doubt, or fear of failure. For example, if you find yourself stuck in a cycle of negative thinking—believing that a setback means you're not cut out for business or that every decision you make could lead to disaster—CBT provides tools to re-frame those thoughts into more realistic and constructive ones. The goal is to break the cycle of negative thinking and replace it with healthier, more balanced perspectives. This shift in mindset can improve decision-making, reduce anxiety, and help you maintain emotional stability even in high-pressure situations.

How Online Therapy Platforms Can Offer Flexible Solutions

For busy entrepreneurs, finding time for therapy can seem daunting, but ***online therapy platforms*** offer ***flexible solutions*** that fit into your schedule. Online therapy is not only convenient, but it also provides more immediate access to care, making it easier to find the right therapist without the logistical barriers of travel or rigid appointment times. For many, this option reduces the stress of scheduling and increases the likelihood of consistent participation in therapy.

Seeking ***therapy or counseling*** is a powerful step in managing the mental health challenges that often come with entrepreneurship. Whether through **talking to a professional who understands business pressures**, using *CBT to manage negative thought patterns*, or utilizing the flexibility of *online therapy platforms*, entrepreneurs can find support that fits their unique needs and busy schedules. Prioritising mental health through therapy not only enhances your personal well-being but also strengthens your ability to lead and grow your business effectively.

Using Peer Support Groups to Share Experiences

Entrepreneurship can often feel like a lonely journey, especially when mental health challenges arise. *Peer support groups* offer a powerful way to connect with others who understand your struggles, creating a space where you can share experiences, gain insights, and find comfort in knowing you're not alone. By engaging with fellow entrepreneurs facing similar challenges, you can reduce feelings of isolation, build emotional resilience, and develop a stronger support network.

Finding Groups for Entrepreneurs with Mental Health Challenges

One of the first steps in leveraging peer support is *finding groups* specifically tailored to entrepreneurs dealing with mental health challenges. These groups can be found through various avenues—local business networks, entrepreneurial hubs, or online platforms focused on mental health. Your GP may also have professional links. Look for communities or groups that focus on the unique pressures entrepreneurs face, such as balancing personal well-being with business demands, handling the isolation of leadership, or managing stress and anxiety. Many organizations now recognize the mental health struggles common among entrepreneurs and offer groups designed to provide mutual support and understanding. By joining a group with like-minded individuals, you'll gain access to a community that not only offers emotional support but also shares practical insights for navigating both business and mental health challenges.

How Sharing with Others Reduces Isolation and Builds Resilience

One of the most powerful aspects of peer support is the realization that you're not alone in your struggles. **Sharing your experiences with others** who truly understand what you're going through can dramatically reduce feelings of isolation. Hearing from peers who have faced similar challenges—whether it's the pressure of decision-making, the fear of failure, or the toll of overwork—can provide validation and relief, knowing that your struggles are not unique. This sense of connection fosters resilience by reminding you that others have faced and overcome similar obstacles, helping you feel supported and capable of doing the same. As you share your own story, you may also find that giving advice or encouragement to others strengthens your own emotional resilience, creating a cycle of mutual support.

The Benefits of Anonymous or Open Discussions with Peers

Peer support groups come in many forms, and **both anonymous and open discussions** offer valuable benefits. Some individuals may feel more comfortable in **anonymous settings**, such as online forums or groups where participants don't have to reveal their identities. These environments allow for open, honest conversations without the fear of judgment or professional repercussions. Anonymous platforms provide a safe space for entrepreneurs who may otherwise feel hesitant to discuss their mental health openly. On the other hand, **open discussions**—whether in-person or virtual—can foster deeper connections and more personal relationships. In these groups, you may develop long-term friendships and mentorship that extend beyond the group, providing ongoing support and guidance. Both formats create an environment where entrepreneurs can share their struggles and successes, offering different ways to connect based on individual comfort levels.

Engaging in **peer support groups** offers a lifeline to entrepreneurs facing mental health challenges. Whether through **finding groups for entrepreneurs**, experiencing the relief of **sharing with others**, or choosing between **anonymous or open discussions**, peer support provides an invaluable opportunity to reduce isolation and build resilience. By connecting with others who understand the unique pressures of entrepreneurship, you can find comfort, support, and a renewed sense of strength in your personal and professional journey.

Developing a Mental Health Action Plan

Taking control of your mental health as an entrepreneur requires not just awareness but a proactive strategy. A **mental health action plan** is a personalized guide that helps you manage your well-being in both the short and long term. It outlines your triggers, coping strategies, and support systems, providing clarity on how to handle stress, anxiety, or depression when they arise. Creating this plan ensures you're prepared for difficult moments and helps you stay on track with your mental health goals over time.

Writing Down Triggers, Coping Strategies, and Emergency Contacts

A key element of any mental health action plan is ***writing down your triggers***—the specific situations, feelings, or stressors that tend to lead to mental health struggles. Whether it's financial uncertainty, decision fatigue, or isolation, identifying what triggers your anxiety, depression, or burnout helps you recognize the early signs of trouble. Once you've identified your triggers, outline ***coping strategies*** that work for you, such as mindfulness exercises, taking breaks, physical activity, or reaching out for support. Having these strategies written down makes it easier to remember what actions to take when you feel overwhelmed. Additionally, include a list of ***emergency contacts***—trusted individuals, such as family members, friends, or mental health professionals, who you can turn to during a mental health crisis. Knowing who to contact in moments of distress can be a vital part of staying safe and supported.

Setting Clear Goals for Managing Mental Health in the Long Term

In addition to addressing immediate challenges, a mental health action plan should include ***clear goals for managing mental health*** over the long term. These goals might include maintaining work-life balance, reducing stress through specific habits, or achieving emotional stability by regularly practicing self-care. Be realistic in setting these goals and break them down into manageable steps. For example, if your goal is to reduce anxiety, you might commit to practicing mindfulness for 10 minutes a day or taking a walk during lunch breaks to clear your mind. By setting these goals, you create a road map that encourages you to actively manage your mental health, rather than only responding when things become difficult. This approach helps you stay committed to your well-being as part of your ongoing routine, rather than treating it as an afterthought.

Establishing Regular Mental Health Check-Ins with a Professional

A critical component of any mental health action plan is ***establishing regular mental health check-ins with a professional***. Whether it's a therapist, counselor, or coach, regular sessions with a mental health professional allow you to track your progress, discuss challenges, and adjust your coping strategies as needed. These check-ins create a structured opportunity to assess how well your plan is working and whether any changes are necessary. Having a professional guide you through the process ensures that you're not navigating your mental health alone and provides accountability for staying consistent with your plan. Even if you're not in crisis, these regular sessions help maintain your mental well-being and prevent smaller issues from becoming bigger problems over time.

Developing a ***mental health action plan*** is an essential step in managing the unique pressures of entrepreneurship. By ***writing down your triggers, coping strategies, and emergency contacts, setting clear goals for long-term well-being***, and ***establishing regular mental health check-ins***, you create a proactive framework to support your mental health journey. This plan ensures that you're prepared to handle challenges as they arise, while also building a foundation for long-term emotional resilience and success.

12

4.1 Cultivating Resilience in the Face of Setbacks

Redefining Failure as a Learning Experience

Failure is an inevitable part of entrepreneurship, but how you respond to it can shape your personal growth and the future success of your business. Instead of viewing failure as a reflection of your worth or ability, it can be redefined as an opportunity for learning and improvement. By embracing a *growth mindset*, analysing setbacks for valuable lessons, and building confidence through small victories, failure becomes a stepping stone rather than a stumbling block.

Shifting from a Fixed to a Growth Mindset

One of the most powerful ways to redefine failure is by *shifting from a fixed to a growth mindset*. A fixed mindset leads you to believe that your abilities and intelligence are static, so when you fail, it can feel like an indictment of your potential. In contrast, a ***growth mindset*** encourages you to view challenges and failures as opportunities to develop new skills and insights. When you adopt this perspective, setbacks become part of the process of growth and innovation, rather than a reason to doubt yourself. By focusing on what you can learn from each failure, you'll approach entrepreneurship with more resilience, curiosity, and an openness to continuous improvement.

How to Analyse Failures for Valuable Lessons

Failure only becomes valuable when you take the time to ***analyse it for lessons***. Instead of brushing off setbacks or dwelling on them negatively, look at each failure as data—what worked, what didn't, and why? Break down the situation to understand the key factors that led to the failure. Was it a lack of preparation? An external factor beyond your control? A flaw in execution or timing? Once you've identified the root cause, you can create strategies to avoid similar mistakes in the future. By seeing failure as a learning tool, you empower yourself to grow both personally and professionally, and you'll be better equipped to handle future challenges.

Building Confidence Through Small, Incremental Wins

Redefining failure also involves **building confidence through small, incremental wins**. Success doesn't have to come in the form of massive achievements—every small victory along the way counts. After a setback, focusing on small, achievable goals helps you regain momentum and rebuild confidence. Each step forward, no matter how small, proves that you're learning, improving, and moving closer to your larger objectives. These incremental wins also shift your focus from dwelling on past failures to recognizing your ability to overcome challenges and make progress. Over time, these small victories accumulate, reinforcing your resilience and helping you build the confidence needed to tackle bigger goals without the fear of failure holding you back.

By ***redefining failure as a learning experience***, you can transform the way you approach setbacks in your entrepreneurial journey. Shifting to a ***growth mindset***, taking time to ***analyse failures for valuable lessons***, and focusing on ***small, incremental wins*** will help you build resilience, learn from your mistakes, and move forward with renewed confidence. Failure is not the end—it's an opportunity for growth and a crucial part of your path to success.

The Importance of Emotional Intelligence in Business

In the fast-paced world of entrepreneurship, ***emotional intelligence (EQ)*** is a crucial skill that can significantly impact both your personal well-being and your business success. Emotional intelligence is the ability to recognize, understand, and manage your own emotions, as well as the emotions of others. Cultivating emotional intelligence allows you to navigate stressful situations with clarity, build stronger relationships, and anticipate potential mental health challenges before they escalate. Here's how developing emotional intelligence can benefit your business and mental health.

Recognizing and Managing Your Emotional Responses to Stress

One of the key components of emotional intelligence is the ability to ***recognize and manage your emotional responses to stress***. Entrepreneurship often involves high levels of uncertainty, financial pressure, and decision-making challenges, all of which can trigger intense emotions. When you're able to recognize early signs of stress—such as frustration, anxiety, or pressure—you can take steps to manage these emotions before they spiral out of control. This might involve stepping away from a stressful situation to take a few deep breaths, practicing mindfulness, or engaging in a quick mental reset. By being aware of how you respond to stress and developing strategies to manage it, you can maintain your focus, make better decisions, and prevent emotional reactions from negatively impacting your business.

How Empathy Can Help Build Better Relationships with Clients and Team Members

Empathy—*the ability to understand and share the feelings of others*—*is a cornerstone of emotional intelligence* and a powerful tool for building stronger relationships with both clients and team members. In business, empathy allows you to see things from another person's perspective, whether it's understanding a client's frustrations or recognizing a team member's need for support. When you approach interactions with empathy, you create a sense of trust and respect, which fosters more positive and productive working relationships. Clients feel heard and valued, making them more likely to stay loyal to your business, and team members are more likely to feel motivated and engaged when they know their emotional well-being is taken into account. Cultivating empathy not only strengthens these relationships but also creates a more supportive and collaborative work environment.

Developing Self-Awareness to Anticipate Mental Health Challenges

At the core of emotional intelligence is *self-awareness*—the ability to recognize and understand your own emotions, thoughts, and behaviours. **Developing self-awareness** can help you anticipate potential mental health challenges before they become overwhelming. For example, if you notice patterns of stress or anxiety creeping in during certain periods—such as before a major launch or when facing financial uncertainty—you can take proactive steps to manage your mental health. This might involve scheduling more self-care, reaching out for support, or adjusting your workload to prevent burnout. By regularly checking in with yourself and being aware of your emotional state, you can prevent mental health challenges from escalating and better manage the pressures of entrepreneurship.

Incorporating **emotional intelligence** into your business approach can have a profound impact on your success and well-being. By **recognizing and managing your emotional responses to stress**, practicing **empathy** to build better relationships, and **developing self-awareness** to anticipate mental health challenges, you'll create a healthier, more productive work environment for both yourself and those around you. Emotional intelligence isn't just about handling emotions—it's about using them as tools for growth, connection, and resilience in your entrepreneurial journey.

Bouncing Back from Burnout or Depressive Episodes

Experiencing **burnout** or a **depressive episode** can be overwhelming, leaving you feeling emotionally drained, mentally fatigued, and uncertain about how to move forward. However, recovering from these periods is not only possible, but it can also be an opportunity to reassess how you manage your business and mental health. By recognizing the early warning signs of burnout, creating a structured recovery plan, and re-entering work mindfully, you can rebuild resilience and prevent future episodes. Here's how to bounce back from burnout or depression and return to work with a healthier, more balanced approach.

Recognizing Early Signs of Burnout to Avoid Spiraling

One of the most important skills in preventing burnout or depression from spiraling out of control is *recognizing the early signs*. Burnout doesn't usually happen overnight—it's the result of prolonged stress, exhaustion, and feeling overwhelmed. Early symptoms include physical fatigue, irritability, difficulty concentrating, loss of motivation, and feelings of cynicism or detachment from your work. When you notice these signs, it's crucial to take immediate action, such as reducing your workload, taking time off, or practicing self-care. By intervening early, you can prevent burnout from escalating into a full-blown crisis and maintain a sense of control over your mental health. Recognizing and addressing these warning signs before they reach a breaking point is key to long-term emotional resilience.

Setting Up Recovery Plans After Periods of Pressure

If you've already reached the point of **burnout or a depressive episode**, setting up a structured **recovery plan** is essential to rebuilding your well-being. Recovery starts with acknowledging that you need time to heal and that pushing through the pain won't lead to lasting improvement. Begin by identifying specific steps you can take to recover, such as taking extended time off, seeking professional help, or re-evaluating your priorities. Incorporate self-care activities like rest, exercise, healthy eating, and mindfulness into your daily routine to support your mental and physical recovery. It's also helpful to reduce or delegate business responsibilities temporarily, allowing you to focus on healing without feeling overwhelmed. Recovery is a gradual process, and having a plan in place ensures that you're taking intentional steps toward regaining your strength and mental clarity.

How to Return to Work Without Rushing Back into Old Habits

Returning to work after burnout or depression can be tricky, especially if you're eager to get back to your routine. However, it's important to **return to work without rushing back into old habits** that may have contributed to burnout in the first place. Start by easing back into your workday—don't take on too many tasks or responsibilities at once. Set clear boundaries around work hours and make time for breaks, self-care, and social connections to maintain balance. Focus on sustainable productivity rather than pushing yourself to meet unrealistic expectations. Additionally, reflect on what led to your burnout or depressive episode and implement changes to avoid falling into the same patterns. Whether it's learning to say no, delegating more tasks, or building in more rest time, prioritise your mental health as much as your business success. This thoughtful approach helps you return to work with a renewed sense of purpose and well-being, rather than slipping back into an unhealthy work routine.

Bouncing back from burnout or a depressive episode requires self-awareness, intentional recovery, and a mindful approach to re-entering work. By **recognizing early signs of burnout**, **setting up a structured recovery plan**, and **returning to work with a focus on new, healthier habits**, you can regain your energy and resilience while protecting yourself from future pressure. Taking the time to heal and re-establish balance not only benefits your mental health but also strengthens your ability to lead with clarity and focus in your entrepreneurial journey.

13

4.2 Redefining Success Beyond Business Metrics

Shifting Focus from Purely Financial Goals to Personal Fulfillment

For many entrepreneurs, the initial drive to start a business often revolves around achieving ***financial success***. While financial stability is undoubtedly important, focusing solely on financial goals can leave you feeling unfulfilled, even when profits are high. Shifting your focus toward ***personal fulfillment***—finding joy in the work itself and aligning your business goals with your values—can lead to deeper satisfaction and well-being. Here's how to balance financial success with a sense of purpose and personal happiness.

4.2 REDEFINING SUCCESS BEYOND BUSINESS METRICS

Finding Satisfaction in the Process, Not Just the Outcome

Entrepreneurship is a long journey filled with both successes and setbacks. Often, we get caught up in waiting for that "big win"—whether it's hitting a revenue target, securing funding, or landing a major client. However, placing all your happiness on these outcomes can leave you feeling empty when those moments pass. Instead, try to *find satisfaction in the process**, in the daily work, problem-solving, and incremental progress that drives your business forward. Enjoy the small wins along the way, appreciate the relationships you build, and celebrate your personal growth as a leader. By focusing on the journey rather than the destination, you can foster a deeper sense of fulfillment that lasts beyond any single achievement.

How Aligning Business Goals with Personal Values Boosts Well-Being

A powerful way to increase personal fulfillment is by *aligning your business goals with your personal values.* When your work reflects what matters most to you—whether it's creativity, social impact, community, or innovation—it becomes more than just a way to generate income. Running a values-driven business brings a sense of purpose and knowing that your work aligns with who you are at your core leads to greater well-being. Take time to reflect on your values and ask yourself if your current business model, goals, and day-to-day activities align with them. If not, consider ways to adjust your approach so that your business feels like an extension of your personal mission. This alignment creates a sense of coherence between your professional and personal life, reducing internal conflict and boosting overall satisfaction.

Embracing Work That Brings Joy, Not Just Profit

While profitability is essential to running a sustainable business, it's also important to ***embrace work that brings you joy***. Focusing on projects, clients, or tasks that energize and inspire you can make your workday feel more rewarding. When your business becomes solely about chasing profits, it can lead to burnout or a sense of disconnect from what originally motivated you. On the other hand, pursuing work that excites you—whether it's launching a passion project, collaborating with like-minded partners, or creating something innovative—fuels creativity and long-term motivation. Profit and fulfillment don't have to be mutually exclusive. By prioritising work that you find meaningful and enjoyable, you're more likely to sustain energy, passion, and joy in your business journey.

Shifting your focus from ***purely financial goals to personal fulfillment*** transforms the way you experience entrepreneurship. By ***finding satisfaction in the process***, ***aligning your business goals with your personal values***, and ***embracing work that brings joy***, you create a more balanced and meaningful approach to your business. This shift allows you to enjoy the journey, stay true to yourself, and build a business that not only succeeds financially but also enriches your life in the process.

Understanding the Difference Between Busy Work and Productive Work

As an entrepreneur, it's easy to get caught up in the whirlwind of daily tasks, but not all work contributes equally to your success. Recognizing the difference between **busy work**—tasks that fill your time without creating real progress—and **productive work**—activities that drive growth and impact—is essential for maximizing your effectiveness. By focusing on tasks that truly move the needle, delegating or eliminating non-essential activities, and making time for creative work that Energised you, you can work smarter, not harder.

How to Identify Tasks That Truly Move the Needle

One of the first steps in separating busy work from productive work is learning how to **identify tasks that truly move the needle**. These are the tasks that directly contribute to the growth of your business, whether that's acquiring new clients, improving your product or service, or developing strategic partnerships. To determine which activities are most impactful, ask yourself: Does this task lead to revenue growth, improve efficiency, or advance my business goals? If not, it might fall into the category of busy work. Productive work often focuses on long-term value creation rather than short-term task completion. Prioritising these high-impact activities ensures that your time is spent on the areas that will have the greatest return on investment, both financially and in terms of business development.

Delegating or Eliminating Non-Essential Activities

Once you've identified which tasks are critical to your success, the next step is to **delegate or eliminate non-essential activities**. Busy work often involves repetitive, administrative, or low-impact tasks that don't require your direct involvement, such as managing emails, scheduling meetings, or handling routine paperwork. These tasks, while necessary, can take up valuable time and energy that could be better spent on strategic initiatives. Consider outsourcing these responsibilities to a virtual assistant, automating processes where possible, or simply cutting them from your to-do list if they don't add significant value. Delegation allows you to focus on what you do best—leading, innovating, and growing your business—while ensuring that smaller tasks are still handled efficiently.

Making Time for Creative Work That Energizes You

Beyond eliminating busy work, it's important to **make time for creative work that energizes you**. Creative work—whether it's brainstorming new ideas, developing innovative products, or engaging in strategic planning—often gets pushed aside in favour of more urgent, day-to-day tasks. However, these creative activities are the lifeblood of long-term business success and personal fulfillment. Set aside dedicated time in your schedule for this kind of work, ensuring that you have the mental space to focus on big-picture thinking and problem-solving. Creative work not only drives business innovation but also helps you stay connected to the passion that led you to start your business in the first place. This balance between high-impact work and creativity can help you maintain energy and motivation over the long term.

Understanding the difference between busy work and productive work is critical for maximizing your impact as an entrepreneur. By ***identifying tasks that truly move the needle***, ***delegating or eliminating non-essential activities***, and ***making time for creative work***, you can free up your time for the work that matters most. This shift in focus allows you to work with greater intention, stay energised, and drive meaningful progress in your business, rather than just staying busy.

Creating a Long-Term Vision That Includes Mental Well-Being

Building a successful business is a long-term commitment, but achieving sustainable success requires more than just focusing on growth and profitability—it also means prioritising your mental and emotional well-being. Crafting a ***long-term vision*** for your business that includes mental health is key to maintaining balance, avoiding burnout, and fostering a fulfilling life. By setting sustainable goals, integrating personal and family priorities into your business plan, and planning regular mental health check-ins, you can create a holistic approach that ensures success both in your business and personal life.

Setting Sustainable Business Goals

The first step in creating a vision that prioritizes mental well-being is ***setting sustainable business goals***. While ambition is essential to entrepreneurship, it's important to pace yourself and set realistic, achievable goals that don't push you to the brink of exhaustion. Consider what growth looks like over the long term rather than focusing on rapid, short-term gains. Sustainable goals should balance business success with your capacity for handling the workload and stress that comes with it. This might involve setting milestones that allow you to grow at a manageable pace, allocating time for rest and recovery, or building flexibility into your plans to adapt to changing circumstances. By prioritising sustainability over rapid growth, you'll protect your mental health while still moving your business forward.

Incorporating Personal and Family Goals into Your Business Plan

A truly balanced long-term vision also involves ***incorporating personal and family goals into your business plan***. Your business should support—not overshadow—your personal life. Start by identifying what's most important to you outside of work, whether that's spending time with family, pursuing hobbies, or maintaining a healthy lifestyle. Then, think about how your business can help facilitate those goals. For example, you might structure your work schedule to prioritise family time, or set up processes that allow you to take vacations without your business suffering. By aligning your business goals with your personal values, you ensure that success isn't defined solely by financial metrics but by how well your business supports the life you want to live. This integration can help you achieve a sense of fulfillment both professionally and personally.

Planning for Regular Mental Health Check-Ins as Part of Your Strategy

One of the most proactive ways to ensure mental well-being over the long term is to *plan for regular mental health check-ins* as part of your business strategy. Just as you track financial performance or operational efficiency, monitoring your mental health should be an ongoing part of your plan. Schedule regular mental health evaluations, whether through therapy, counseling, or personal reflection, to assess how you're coping with the demands of running a business. These check-ins can help you identify early signs of stress, anxiety, or burnout, allowing you to make adjustments before they escalate. You can also integrate wellness practices like mindfulness, exercise, or stress management techniques into your routine, ensuring that mental well-being is prioritized just as much as business success.

Creating a long-term vision that includes mental well-being ensures that your business supports a balanced, fulfilling life rather than becoming a source of pressure. By *setting sustainable business goals*, *incorporating personal and family priorities*, and *planning for regular mental health check-ins*, you can create a future where success means thriving in both your personal and professional life. This holistic approach enables you to enjoy the journey of entrepreneurship while maintaining the mental clarity and resilience needed for sustained success.

14

4.3 Sustaining Mental Health for the Long Haul

Maintaining Support Networks as Your Business Grows

As your business expands, the challenges you face may become more complex, but maintaining strong *support networks* can provide the stability and guidance you need to navigate these changes. Whether through mentors, peers, mental health professionals, or entrepreneurial communities, having a reliable network is essential for both your business success and personal well-being. As your responsibilities increase, staying connected to these support systems can help you maintain perspective, manage stress, and find the help you need when facing new challenges.

Keeping in Touch with Mentors, Peers, and Mental Health Professionals

As your business grows, it's important to stay **in touch with mentors, peers, and mental health professionals** who have supported you along the way. These relationships are invaluable, providing advice, encouragement, and emotional support. Your mentors can offer insight based on their own experiences, helping you make informed decisions and avoid common pitfalls. Peers who are also navigating entrepreneurship can serve as sounding boards for ideas, frustrations, and successes, providing camaraderie in a way that only fellow business owners can. Equally important, mental health professionals can help you manage stress, maintain emotional resilience, and stay grounded as your business evolves. Make it a priority to regularly connect with these key individuals, whether through scheduled check-ins, informal meetings, or therapy sessions, to ensure that you have consistent support as you face new challenges.

Continuing to Participate in Entrepreneurial Communities

Even as your business demands more of your time, **continuing to participate in entrepreneurial communities** is crucial for maintaining your support network. These communities—whether they're local business groups, online forums, or mastermind circles—provide opportunities to exchange ideas, share resources, and learn from others who are facing similar challenges. As your business grows, your involvement in these groups helps you stay connected to a network of peers who understand the unique pressures of entrepreneurship. It's also a great way to stay informed about industry trends, expand your professional circle, and develop collaborative relationships. By staying engaged in these communities, you can continue learning, growing, and feeling supported as your business scales.

Learning How to Ask for Help as Your Responsibilities Increase

As your business grows, so do your responsibilities, and learning ***how to ask for help*** becomes more critical than ever. While it's natural to want to maintain control over every aspect of your business, trying to handle everything on your own can lead to burnout and inefficiency. Reaching out for support—whether it's delegating tasks to your team, hiring new staff, or seeking advice from your network—is a sign of strength, not weakness. Recognize when you're feeling overwhelmed and be proactive in asking for help before the pressure becomes unmanageable. This can mean asking for guidance on a specific challenge, seeking emotional support when stress levels rise, or relying on your team to handle tasks that are outside your immediate expertise. Cultivating a mindset that embraces collaboration and support will allow you to focus on what you do best, while ensuring that your business continues to thrive without putting unnecessary strain on your mental health.

Maintaining support networks as your business grows is vital for your long-term success and well-being. By ***keeping in touch with mentors, peers, and mental health professionals***, ***continuing to participate in entrepreneurial communities***, and ***learning how to ask for help*** as your responsibilities increase, you can ensure that you're never facing the challenges of entrepreneurship alone. These networks provide the guidance, encouragement, and support needed to navigate the complexities of growing a business while maintaining your personal health and happiness.

Preventing Relapse into Unhealthy Patterns

As an entrepreneur, it's easy to fall back into **unhealthy patterns** when stress levels rise or responsibilities increase. To sustain long-term success and mental well-being, it's crucial to actively monitor your habits, recognize early warning signs of burnout, and adjust your approach as circumstances change. Preventing a relapse into unhealthy patterns requires consistent self-awareness and a commitment to prioritising your mental and emotional health, even as your business grows.

Monitoring Your Stress Levels and Adjusting Workloads as Needed

One of the most effective ways to prevent a relapse into unhealthy habits is by **monitoring your stress levels** and **adjusting your workload** when necessary. As your business evolves, so do the demands placed on your time and energy. Pay attention to how these demands affect your stress levels and overall well-being. If you notice that you're feeling overwhelmed, irritable, or exhausted, it's a sign that adjustments are needed. This might involve delegating tasks to your team, postponing non-essential projects, or simply taking a step back to rest and recharge. Regularly assessing your workload and making conscious adjustments will help you stay balanced and prevent burnout before it becomes unmanageable.

Revisiting Coping Strategies and Adjusting Them as Circumstances Change

Coping strategies that worked for you in the past might need to be revisited and adjusted as your circumstances change. What helped you manage stress at one stage of your business may not be as effective at another. Take the time to ***revisit your coping strategies*** and ensure they're still serving you. If certain techniques—like mindfulness, exercise, or time management—are no longer effective, explore new approaches that fit your current needs. For example, if your business has grown and your schedule has become more demanding, you might need to incorporate shorter, more frequent breaks or shift to a different type of relaxation practice. Flexibility in your coping strategies ensures that you can adapt to new challenges without reverting to unhealthy habits.

Recognizing Early Warning Signs and Acting Before Burnout Hits

Perhaps the most crucial part of preventing a relapse into unhealthy patterns is ***recognizing early warning signs*** and taking action before burnout hits. These warning signs can manifest in many forms, including persistent fatigue, loss of motivation, increased irritability, or trouble focusing. When you notice these signs, don't wait for them to escalate. Instead, act quickly by adjusting your workload, reaching out for support, or prioritising self-care. Taking proactive steps at the first sign of trouble can prevent a full-blown burnout episode and keep you on track. The earlier you intervene, the easier it is to regain balance and avoid slipping back into unproductive patterns.

Preventing relapse into unhealthy patterns is an ongoing process that requires self-awareness, flexibility, and proactive action. By ***monitoring your stress levels***, ***revisiting coping strategies***, and ***recognizing early warning signs***, you can maintain a healthy balance between your personal well-being and your business responsibilities. These practices not only help you avoid burnout but also enable you to sustain long-term success while preserving your mental and emotional health.

Ongoing Self-Care and Personal Growth

As your business evolves, so too should your approach to ***self-care and personal growth***. The demands of entrepreneurship shift over time, and your self-care routine needs to adapt accordingly to ensure that your mental, emotional, and physical well-being remain a priority. Beyond business success, investing in your personal development and celebrating your mental health progress are essential for maintaining a fulfilling and balanced life.

Continuing to Evolve Your Self-Care Routine as Your Business Changes

Your *self-care routine* is not static—it needs to grow and change as your business does. What worked for you in the early stages of your entrepreneurial journey might not be sufficient as your responsibilities increase or your business expands. Take the time to regularly reassess your self-care practices. For example, if your workload has intensified, you may need to incorporate more restorative activities, such as mindfulness or stretching, or take longer breaks to recover. Alternatively, if your stressors have shifted, you might need different forms of support, such as joining a mastermind group or engaging in therapy. By staying in tune with your evolving needs and adjusting your routine accordingly, you ensure that your self-care keeps pace with your business growth.

Investing in Personal Development Outside of Business Skills

While building your business skills is important, *investing in personal development* beyond the professional sphere is key to holistic growth. This could involve learning new hobbies, engaging in creative pursuits, or working on your emotional intelligence. Personal development can take many forms—whether it's improving your communication skills, deepening your self-awareness, or cultivating healthier relationships. By developing areas outside of your business, you not only enrich your life but also foster resilience, creativity, and well-being. Personal growth strengthens your ability to lead, adapt, and handle challenges, making you a more balanced and effective entrepreneur. Remember, your success is not defined solely by your business achievements but also by how much you grow as an individual.

Celebrating Your Progress and Milestones in Mental Health

One of the most empowering aspects of ongoing self-care is *celebrating your progress* in mental health and personal growth. It's easy to focus on what still needs improvement, but taking time to acknowledge how far you've come is essential for maintaining a positive mindset. Whether it's overcoming burnout, achieving better work-life balance, or simply managing stress more effectively, these milestones deserve recognition. Celebrating your progress reinforces your commitment to self-care and helps build confidence in your ability to prioritise your well-being. Create moments to reflect on your mental health journey—whether through journaling, treating yourself to something special, or sharing your wins with a trusted friend or mentor. These celebrations not only honour your growth but also inspire continued focus on maintaining and improving your mental health.

Ongoing self-care and personal growth are critical components of a balanced and fulfilling entrepreneurial journey. By *evolving your self-care routine* as your business changes, *investing in personal development* beyond business skills, and *celebrating your mental health milestones*, you ensure that both your business and personal life thrive. This continuous focus on self-improvement and well-being supports long-term success, resilience, and happiness in every area of your life.

15

Moving Forward with Balance and Strength

As you reach the conclusion of this book, I want to take a moment to summarize some of the key points we've explored together. Running a business is no small feat, and the mental and emotional challenges that come with entrepreneurship are real and often underappreciated. But by acknowledging these challenges and taking proactive steps to care for your mental health, you can build not only a successful business but also a fulfilling life.

We've discussed the importance of recognizing ***early signs of burnout*** and the necessity of developing ***coping strategies*** tailored to your personal and professional needs. We explored how creating boundaries between your work and personal life, delegating tasks, and building a strong support network can help you maintain balance as your business grows. We emphasized the importance of ***self-care***, not just in moments of crisis, but as an ongoing practice that evolves alongside your business. And most importantly, we looked at how shifting your mindset—whether by redefining failure or focusing on long-term mental well-being—can transform the way you approach both work and life.

Throughout these chapters, the central message has been clear: **you matter**. Your mental health is not an afterthought—it's a fundamental part of your entrepreneurial journey. By prioritising your well-being, you set yourself up for long-term success, both personally and professionally.

I want to thank you for taking the time to read this book and for investing in your mental health. Whether you're just starting out or deep into your entrepreneurial journey, I hope these insights have resonated with you and provided useful tools for managing the unique pressures of running a business. Should you like to reach out, you are welcome to email me at nzcornerstore@gmail.com

If this book has been helpful to you, I would be truly grateful if you could take a moment to *leave a review on Amazon*. Your feedback not only helps me improve but also enables other entrepreneurs to discover the book and find the support they need.

Thank you again for joining me on this journey, and remember: you have the strength to manage your mind while growing your business. Here's to your continued success and well-being!

If you would like early notification of upcoming titles, or simply to reach out, you can contact me at: nzcornerstore@gmail.com

Justin Thyme - New Zealand

www.ingramcontent.com/pod-product-compliance
Lightning Source LLC
Chambersburg PA
CBHW050324230526
45471CB00005B/2339